CORPORATE RELATIONS

Also by Jena Osman:
Public Figures (Wesleyan Press, 2012)
The Network (Fence Books, 2010)
An Essay in Asterisks (Roof Books, 2004)
The Character (Beacon Press, 1999)

Jena Osman

CORPORATE RELATIONS

Burning Deck/Anyart, Providence

Acknowledgments:

Versions and excerpts of this project have appeared in *The Rumpus, P-Queue, Chicago Review, Colorado Review* and on a Fact-Simile trading card; thanks to the editors. Thanks to Jennifer Clayton Gelman for lawyerly advice. Thanks to the Howard Foundation, Temple University, and the MacDowell Colony for the time. Thanks to Justices Keith and Rosmarie Waldrop for their majority opinion in Poets United v. the Stopwatch Commission.

The image on p. 47 is from "Exhibits in connection with Brief of the City of Scranton, Intervenor" used as evidence in the 1922 case Pennsylvania Coal Company v. Mahon.

Cover image by Amze Emmons, cover type and design by Neil Cleary-Trask.

Burning Deck is the literature program of Anyart: Contemporary Arts Center, a tax-exempt (501c3), non-profit organization.

© 2014 by Jena Osman
ISBN13: 978-1-936194-17-9, original paperback

CONTENTS

The Beautiful Life of Persona Ficta   11

First Amendment Rights   13
    First National Bank of Boston v. Bellotti   15
    A Mouth   18
    Pacific Gas & Electric Co. v. Public Utilities Commission   19
    Gag Order   22
    Citizens United v. Federal Election Commission   23
    Manchurian Candidate   27

Fourth Amendment Rights   29
    Hale v. Henkel   31
    Security   33
    Marshall v. Barlow's   34
    The Border   37

Fifth Amendment Rights   39
    Noble v. Union River Logging Railroad Company   41
    Mechanized Eccentric   43
    Pennsylvania Coal Company v. Mahon   44
    Scientific Management   48
    Fong Foo v. United States   49
    Malaprops   52

Sixth and Seventh Amendment Rights   53
    Armour Packing Company v. United States   55
    Animals 1   57
    Ross v. Bernhard   58
    Animals 2   61

Fourteenth Amendment Rights 63
    Santa Clara v. Southern Pacific Railroad 65
    We 68
    Chicago, Milwaukee and St. Paul Railway v. Minnesota 69
    Industrial Palace 71

Two Notes 73
Appendix 75
Further Reading 77
Biographical Note 79

Our path leads through the poetry of machines, from the bungling citizen to the perfect electric man.
—Dziga Vertov

I cannot tell what the future will force upon us, but I respectfully dissent from this judgment today.
—David Souter

CORPORATE RELATIONS

THE BEAUTIFUL LIFE OF PERSONA FICTA

a corporation is to a person as a person is to a machine
> friends of the court we know them as good and bad, they too are sheep and goats ventriloquizing the ghostly fiction.

a corporation is to a body as a body is to a puppet
> putting it in caricature, if there are natural persons then there are those who are not that, buying candidates. there are those who are strong on the ground and then weak in the air. weight shifts to the left leg while the propaganda arm extends.

a corporation is to an individual as an individual is to an uncanny valley
> the separation of individual wills from collective wills, magic words. they create an eminent body that is different from their own selves. reach over with the open palm of the left and force to the right while pamphlets disengage.

a corporation has convictions as a person has mechanical parts
> making a hash of this statute, the state is a body. Dobson Hobson and Jobson are masquerading under an alias. push off with the right foot, and at the same time step forward with the left foot. childlike voice complements visual cues and contributes to cuteness factor of the contestational robot.

a corporation has likes and dislikes as a body has shareholders
> bound by precedents the spectral then showed himself for what he was, a blotch to public discourse. the right foot is immediately brought forward. the body flattens toward the deck rather than leap into the air. it is not a hop. subversive literature engaged.

a corporation gives birth as a natural human births profit margins
> some really weird interpretations fully panoplied for war, a myth. torso breaks slightly forward. the hand is not entirely supine, but sloping from the thumb about thirty degrees. head rotation and sonar sensing technologies are employed to create believable movement, while allowing for only the most limited interaction.

a corporation has an enthusiasm for ethical behavior as a creature has economic interests only
> facial challenges. this person which is not a human being. not a physical personality of mankind. custom built from aluminum stock.

a corporation is we the people as a person is a cog
> a funny kind of thing, naïve shareholders. where there is property there is no personality. take off in full stride. lead leg exaggerates the knee lift of a normal stride. cordless microphones, remote control systems, hidden tape recorders.

a corporation has a conscience as a body has a human likeness
> forceful lily; so difficult to tell the two apart. paralyze the wheels of industry. an insatiable monster, soulless and conscienceless, a fund.

a corporation says hey I'm talking to you, as an individual speaks through a spokesperson
> they wear a scarlet letter that says "C" rejecting a century of history. the strong over the weak. better armed. supernatural. richer. more numerous. these are the facts.

a corporation admires you from afar and then has the guts to approach you and ask you for your number, as a being activates a cognitive mechanism for selecting mates
> it is a nightmare that Congress endorsed. mega-corporation as human group, the realm of hypothesis.

a corporation warms the bed and wraps its arms around you and just wants to spoon as a natural human wants to organize profits
> it's overbroad, a glittering generality, a fiction to justify the power of the strong invented by prophets of force. there were narrower paths to incorporeal rights.

a corporation has upstanding character as a body has photorealistic texture
> the absorptive powers of some prehistoric sponge. there are good fictions and bad fictions. can the fiction ever disappear?

FIRST AMENDMENT RIGHTS

FIRST NATIONAL BANK OF BOSTON v. BELLOTTI

the rights of the listener

        limiting the stock of information

                mental exploration

a megaphone

today, I will address the mootness question

                what will happen in the future

I certainly hope so your honor, they owe me some money

the corporation can not have opinions   that is unanimous

money is speech and speech is protected

        it cannot squelch

    the right of the public to hear

1976. Massachusetts voters were to consider a ballot question regarding whether their flat tax should be replaced by a progressive income tax. First National Bank of Boston and a consortium of major corporations wanted to take out media ads arguing against the referendum; they felt the graduated tax would be bad for business. However, a Massachusetts statute prevented corporations from spending money to influence the vote. The corporations argued that this statute denied them their First Amendment right to free speech; since they don't have mouths, advertising is the only means for making their opinions known. The Supreme Court majority decided that the Massachusetts statute should in fact be overturned—not so much because corporations have the right to free speech, but because the statute prevented humans from hearing all sides of the debate. The right of free speech was interpreted as the right of the listener to *hear* speech, no matter what the source. This decision opened the door for corporations to speak (i.e. spend money) in order to influence politics.

it is an irrational device

        I have a little problem Mr. Fox

"Mr. Corporation, you should not be running newspapers, you should be selling shoes."

one must first pass through the person loophole

                you first have to show you are a person

there is a flat sentence

that is not an imaginary evil

                            their views may drown

    the States are free to define the rights of their creatures

the First Amendment does not "belong" to any definable category of persons

the very heart

"A corporation is an artificial being, invisible, intangible, and existing only in contemplation of law." (Trustees of Dartmouth College v. Woodward, 1819, quoted by Justice Rehnquist, dissenting)

A MOUTH

no mouth
a human person torn down from the platform
permission to speak denied
within the free flow of ideas
shutting off the sound by means of different positions of the tongue and jaws
forcing it explosively against the hard palate
a movable floor made up of the tongue and lower jaw
theory of the vocal bomb

when the mouth is closed the tongue comes in close contact with the roof
communication impeded by a curtain of flesh, the soft palate
the throat and the mouth in distinct chambers
keep the muscles of the lips and face immovable
the ventriloquial drone

were it not for this tendency to lobby, there would be no such thing as ventriloquism
the voice appears to come from various points and not from the actual speaker
teeth closed and lips only slightly parted
placing a hand at the back of the political neck or within the hollow congressional body and moving a lever with the thumb
voice thrown

standing before a mirror, close the lips, keep the jaws rigid
bring the teeth together and stretch the tongue until it touches the roof
of the mouth near the back of the front upper teeth

Vent.   "What did he try you for?"
O.L.   "Cuz I made a speech."
Vent.   "What, you made a speech! What did you say?"

PACIFIC GAS & ELECTRIC CO v. PUBLIC UTILITIES COMMISSION

envelope space

the envelope

the envelope has never been open to the public

        an enforced right of excess…access…calls for some mechanism

it is the death or die or whatever
no, it is not the death or die

the right to speak also necessarily includes the right not to speak
the extra space

Mr. Harris: Doesn't belong to the utility.
Unidentified Justice: Yes.
Mr. Harris: Sorry.
Unidentified Justice. Yes.

the First Amendment cannot depend upon a metaphysical definition of space

        we are talking about who gets a free ride on that space

the forced compulsion to speak when we prefer not to speak
live free or die

it is kind of an insult

1986. Pacific Gas & Electric, which had a monopoly in its region, issued a newsletter called *Progress*. The newsletter provided energy tips, as well as particular views on energy policy. A consumer advocacy group, Toward Utility Rate Normalization (TURN) stated that utility bill envelopes should not be used to distribute political editorials; customers should not have to bear the cost of the company's political speech. The California Public Utilities Commission ruled that the envelope space was ratepayer's property and in order to even the playing field, permitted TURN to use that "extra space" four times a year for its own newsletter. The Supreme Court decided that this ruling violated the electrical utility's First Amendment free speech rights, which included the right not to be associated with statements with which it disagreed.

could you compel them to carry an advertisement from the sun people

      to carry something that they don't want to carry?

did it use the word "neutral"?
that is your word?
that is my word
your honor, any message is not a neutral message
do you know anything today in the public view that is neutral?

you have a good many hypotheticals posed to you this afternoon

you suggest that a tornado is different
it would chill its own speech

the side of every building, the surface of every gas holder rising above our cities, and the bumpers of every utility vehicle

      excess space

strains the rationale beyond breaking point

"To ascribe to such artificial entities an 'intellect' or 'mind' for freedom of conscience purposes is to confuse metaphor with reality." (Justice Rehnquist, dissenting)

GAG ORDER

A story. Descartes constructed an automaton he named Francine. During a sea voyage, Francine was discovered in a box by the ship's captain. She was so real, the captain threw her overboard.

Wooden clockwork man with moving eyes and mouth. German, 18th century. Height: 59 cm.

A pretty automaton Mercury moves in accordance with the company's wishes and can reply 'yes' or 'no' to questions.

A grocer's stall with a mechanical shopkeeper seated behind the counter.

Having poured liquid from a bottle into a glass, he raises his arm and drinks it down, rolling his eyes with appreciation.

Beautifully sculpted features and eyes which move, worked from within their hollow skulls.

A mechanism causes her to move her head and eyes, give a slight bow and breathe 'naturally' by a rising and falling motion of her bosom.

He has a very well carved head of wood complete with beard.

Descartes believed that a machine could perfectly duplicate the lower animals but that no machine could replicate human speech convincingly.

it is quite impossible to ventriloquize a whisper
a downward movement pulls the mouth open
by means of a picture wire
or gut string,
a spring
causing the jaw to close
as the wire is relaxed
a slot in the back of the head

CITIZENS UNITED v. FEDERAL ELECTION COMMISSION

a narrowly tailored remedy to that interest

        to use the words of one Justice, that is ventriloquist-speak

        I would say that it is more like surrogate speech

Justice Ginsburg: who is the "you"?

people think that representatives are being bought, okay?

the line dissolves on practical application

it is said the distinction requires the use of magic words

        the words of the statute were "any person"

—the Earth is not—

Chief Justice Roberts: Why don't you tell us now.
We will give you time for rebuttal.
[Laughter]
Justice Scalia: Don't keep us in suspense.
[Laughter]

as if we have an unbroken amount of years

        a blotch to public discourse

    we gave some really weird interpretations

                    if it has to lose, the answer is yes

                    a hierarchy of bases

2010. Citizens United, a conservative organization, wanted to advertise and air a film critical of potential Democratic presidential candidate Hillary Clinton through free video-on-demand during primary season. In anticipation that the Federal Election Commission would prohibit the broadcast on the grounds that the film constituted a corporate "electioneering communication," and was therefore illegal under the Bipartisan Campaign Reform Act, Citizens United proactively sought injunctive relief from the ban. The issue at hand was not a constitutional question; however, during argument, members of the Supreme Court majority actively changed the terms of the case to hinge around free speech and decided that limits on corporate (and union) campaign expenditures are a suppression of speech. The dissenting opinion, written by Justice Souter, accused Chief Justice Roberts of violating Court procedures. In response, the Chief Justice agreed to have the case reargued—a rare occurrence. Elena Kagan, just confirmed as Solicitor General, presented the government's case and lost. Corporations are now free to speak via unlimited funding of electioneering communications, although they cannot directly contribute to candidates' coffers. Justice Souter retired from the bench before the case was reargued; his dissent is not available to the public, essentially erased from the record.

there is no place where an ongoing chill is more dangerous

we couldn't sever it based on the language

presumably as a poison pill

these corporations have a lot of money

        we get to that when we get there

                              they want winners

individuals are more complicated than that

Chief Justice Roberts: You have a busy job.
You can't expect everybody to do that.
[Laughter]

is that a yes?
is that a yes?

you are not talking about the railroad barons and the rapacious trusts

      they wear a scarlet letter that says C
      but it is a nightmare that Congress endorsed

is there any distinction that Congress could draw between corporations
and natural human beings

the courts who created corporations as persons, gave birth to
corporations as persons
      the Court imbued a creature of State law with human characteristics

   few of us are only our economic interests
      we have beliefs, we have convictions, we have likes and dislikes

individuals are more complicated than that

muffled the voices
suppressing the speech of manifold corporations
prevents their voices from reaching the public

      this is simply a matter of legislative grace
                            it follows (as night the day)

that glittering generality

"…corporations have no consciences, no beliefs, no feelings, no thoughts, no desires. Corporations help structure and facilitate the activities of human beings, to be sure, and their 'personhood' often serves as a useful legal fiction. But they are not themselves members of 'We the People' by whom and for whom our Constitution was established." (Justice Stevens, dissenting)

MANCHURIAN CANDIDATE

the words of constructed actors
from narrow to broad
flat transformation figures
slapped into bankruptcy

a straight piece of wire driven through the side of the face
from cheek to cheek
a spiral spring strong enough to pull the mouth shut smartly
after being opened by a tug on the picture wire below
a wire is driven through the neck stick
the head readily removable for packing

the queen of diamonds triggers your speech

an uncertain drone, finally settling down to a clear sustained hum
when you hear that distant-sounding drone
you know that you have your mouth as it should be
transition from the drone to the natural voice
the sound of the word as given by the drone would seem good enough

when you are ready to try this voice in public
take your position as far from the company as possible

FOURTH AMENDMENT RIGHTS

HALE v. HENKEL

he might criminate himself as he avers

and your petitioner will ever pray

                        failed and refused, and still fails and refuses

I shall have to respectfully decline to answer
I shall give the same answer to that
I shall repeat the answer as given before
The same answer to that question
I give the same answer to that question
I must decline to answer for the reason stated

I just wish to state that I have declined to answer the questions, with the utmost respect

                  has the matter been put in such shape?

1906. In pursuing a potential anti-trust case against a group of tobacco corporations, a federal grand jury ordered Edwin Hale to produce an extensive set of documents. He refused. On its own accord, the Supreme Court defended Hale's refusal on the grounds that the corporation he worked for (MacAndrews & Forbes) was entitled to protection under the Fourth Amendment and that an overbroad subpoena for corporate documents constituted an unreasonable search and seizure.

I have now here the body of the said Edwin F. Hale, as by the said writ I am commanded

                it is this which gives to the proceeding its color of oppression

to enter a man's house
by virtue of a nameless warrant
in order to produce evidence
is worse than the Spanish Inquisition

                                        the minds of the framers

compelling a man to be a witness against himself

                            look behind the corporate form and discover

organizing itself as a collective body

                                              aggregated capital
the source of nearly all great enterprises

        it is difficult to say
        how its business could be carried on
        denuded of this mass of material

a corporation
                not part of the "People"
                nor is it embraced by the word "persons"

to this I am not prepared to assent.

"Citizens" is a descriptive word

a collective and changing body of men

persons politic and incorporate

"It may be that it is the obnoxious thing in its mildest and least repulsive form; but illegitimate and unconstitutional practices get their first footing in that way…" (Justice Brewer, dissenting)

SECURITY

a fit of confiscation
a puppet seizure

a figure free of strings
head in diving bell
or face behind gas mask

reads your mail
taps your phone
tracks your chip
sifts your words
through an algorithm

automated surveillance system
free of consciousness

set in motion by your operator
loose joints at knees and elbows
strings at the wrists

MARSHALL v. BARLOW'S

"reasonable"

                                       "unreasonable"

I do not have it at fingertip
I'll have it when I return to the lectern

Worst First Program Scheduling Guide

rank in producing disabling accidents
                                       he's just bugging me

I would be bootstrapping if I did that

a company town,
                an "economic anachronism"

just walked in off the street and said "I'd like to look at your plant"

there is a constant shifting back and forth

1978. The Occupational Safety and Health Act empowered federal inspectors to search any employment facility within the Act's jurisdiction for hazards and violations that might put public safety at risk. On the morning of September 11, 1975, an OSHA inspector entered the customer service area of Barlow's, Inc., an electrical and plumbing installation business in Pocatello, Idaho. The president and general manager, Ferrol G. "Bill" Barlow, was on hand. The inspector, after showing his credentials, informed Mr. Barlow that he wished to conduct a search of the working areas of the business. Mr. Barlow inquired whether any complaint had been received about his company. The inspector answered no; Barlow's, Inc. had simply turned up in the agency's random selection process. Mr. Barlow demanded to see a search warrant, even though warrants were not required for OSHA inspections. When the inspector could not provide one, Mr. Barlow refused him entry on the grounds that the Fourth Amendment protected the business from an unwarranted search. The Supreme Court ruled in Barlow's favor.

one could move to quash the warrant

is this a search or an inspection?
I take the position that they are synonymous

is it anything more than an eyeball search?

it is that word "reasonable" that has been zeroed in on

you have a thin slice that runs through all of industry

                              a particular paint factory

I stand corrected Your Honor
I think that is correct

a balancing test

Justice Burger: Suppose the Immigration Service asked the OSHA people to let one of the Immigration officials go along with him in let's say the southwestern states where illegal aliens, or whatever states illegal aliens are thought be more frequently working, and then acting on his observations checked on the blue card or green card, or whatever it is the legal alien must have for employment. Would you think that would be permitted under this procedure?

turn on a switch in a ventilating booth

                    furnaces explode and there are fires and people trip and fall in their bathtubs, and so on...

    regrettably, we are unable to agree

                the colonists' experience with the writs of assistance
          agents of the King to search at large for smuggled goods

the businessman

the businessman

    a full arsenal of governmental regulation

the advantages of surprise

                speedy alteration or disguise

    a time lapse

      the issuance of a "new fangled warrant"—to use Mr. Justice Clark's characteristically expressive term

                          futile trips

this purpose is not served by the newfangled

    private interest in being free

"Our constitutional fathers were not concerned about warrantless searches, but about overreaching warrants. It is perhaps too much to say that they feared the warrant more than the search, but it is plain enough that the warrant was the prime object of their concern." (Justice Stevens, dissenting)

THE BORDER

the guard motions you forward

artificial parts caught by the scanner
glow blue
body-powered hook
mechatronic arm

you are wanded
keyed into an engine

a letter or syllable tacked on like an arm
made to specifications
vector prehensor
adjustable grip force
pin and slot
bevel gears and a pulley

discovery of enhancement
proportion, flexibility, lightness
finger driven by the pinion
robogrip pliers

just a stand-in, a carrier, a mule

swabs are taken

weightless
not afflicted with matter's inertia
biometric control scheme
motive torque

as thoughts grow dimmer
go around, from the circle
out of the car for the pat-down

FIFTH AMENDMENT RIGHTS

NOBLE v. UNION RIVER LOGGING RAILROAD COMPANY

1893. The Union River Logging Railroad, because of its status as a railroad company, had federal approval for right of way through public land. Later, the Secretary of the Interior concluded that Union River was actually more of a logging company and rescinded the right of way. Union River sought an injunction against that decision because the company was denied its Fifth Amendment right to due process. The Supreme Court agreed to the injunction.

when a public officer
violates the rights of a citizen
equity has jurisdiction to interfere by injunction

...from tide water in Lynch's cove
at the head of Hood's canal

logs, piles, poles, lumber, timber
annulling and canceling maps

a common carrier of passengers
but in the transportation of logs

the action of the former secretary
made improvidently and on false suggestions

the profile of the road
imposed by fraudulent representations

the seizure and possession of the res
with the bailiwick in a proceeding rem

identifying swamp lands, making lists thereof,
and issuing patents therefore

it was not competent for the secretary of the interior

(no dissent on record)

MECHANIZED ECCENTRIC

hunting for a man
a man is capable of doing more work
a man of the mentally sluggish type
a man who was well suited to his job
the maximum work that a man could do on a short spurt
heavy labor on a first-class man
more narrow or wooden a man

a man holding a hammer
a man competing with a steam drill
a man striking fire
hammer ring hammer ring
hammer my fool self to death

in order to do the work in the quickest time,
at what cutting speed shall I run my machine? and
what feed shall I use?

the pulling power and the speed and feed changes of the machine
the metal-cutting machines demanding appeal
put new pulleys on the countershaft of the machine
the speed boss sees that the machine is run
enable the machine to finish its product

a steel driver that struck steel
listen to that cold steel
ring on the rails

PENNSYLVANIA COAL COMPANY v. MAHON

surface-level

                                            below-surface level

surface rights
              bound by valid covenant

under private dwellings or streets or cities
                                            police powers

"if regulation goes too far it will be recognized as a taking"

1922. In 1878, Pennsylvania Coal Company deeded surface property to H.J. Mahon, with the understanding that the company would maintain full rights to remove the coal below. In 1921 the state of Pennsylvania passed the Kohler Act, which prohibited miners from extracting below-surface coal that supported surface-level buildings. When Pennsylvania Coal notified Mahon that it would mine coal beneath his property, Mahon filed suit to prohibit mining in accordance with the Kohler Act. Pennsylvania Coal contended that the Takings Clause of the Fifth Amendment protected its contractual rights to the coal; the Kohler Act takes the property of the Coal Company without due process of law. The Supreme Court agreed: "so far as private persons or communities have seen fit to take the risk of acquiring only surface rights, we cannot see that the fact that their risk has become a danger warrants the giving to them greater rights than they bought."

The World Theatre, Scranton, PA, wrecked by a mine cave shortly after the audience had been dismissed for the night.

to live on the surface over air

    to remove coal without disturbing the surface
                Shylock's right to his pound of flesh

        a vivid preamble

                incontinently projected into unexpected abysses

Extensive timbering being done to save the home of Mr. Prosser of Scranton after a mine cave dropped and he was engulfed in a deep mine cave pit.

        the framers knew full well
whose right of subjacent support had been withheld or waived

            the right to perpetual use of this coal

Another family driven into the street as a result of a mine cave such as menaces the life of the people in the anthracite region.

        the interest of the surface owner in his property
        and of the surface dweller in his own safety

second mining, or the removal of pillars

territory underlaid with anthracite
                the large num-
           ber of people living upon its
           surface

While responding to a fire alarm, William Frey, of Taylor, Pa., near Scranton, Pa., a truck driver, just missed dropping the fire fighting apparatus into this 30-foot pit on a main thoroughfare. Quick action on the part of the driver saved the lives of these firefighters.

                  every pound of coal

even if it were possible to remove whole cities from their present locations

A concrete block apartment in Scranton, PA., collapses as a result of a mine cave at 1 o'clock in the morning, driving all occupants into the street.

cities are built where nature affords

        to prevent the disastrous results of his necessity or folly

                his brickyard…his livery stable…his billiard hall…
his oleomargarine factory

The last resting place of a well known Scranton, PA., woman, whose grave was torn open a few weeks after burial, by a mine cave, in Cathedral Cemetery, where hundreds of bodies have been dropped into the mine beneath. The casket is shown in the pit, torn asunder, and the hand of the corpse is seen protruding from the burial case.

"But restriction imposed to protect the public health, safety or morals from dangers threatened is not a taking. The restriction here in question is merely the prohibition of a noxious use." (Justice Brandeis, dissenting)

GRAVES OF THE DEAD ROCKED BY MINE CAVES

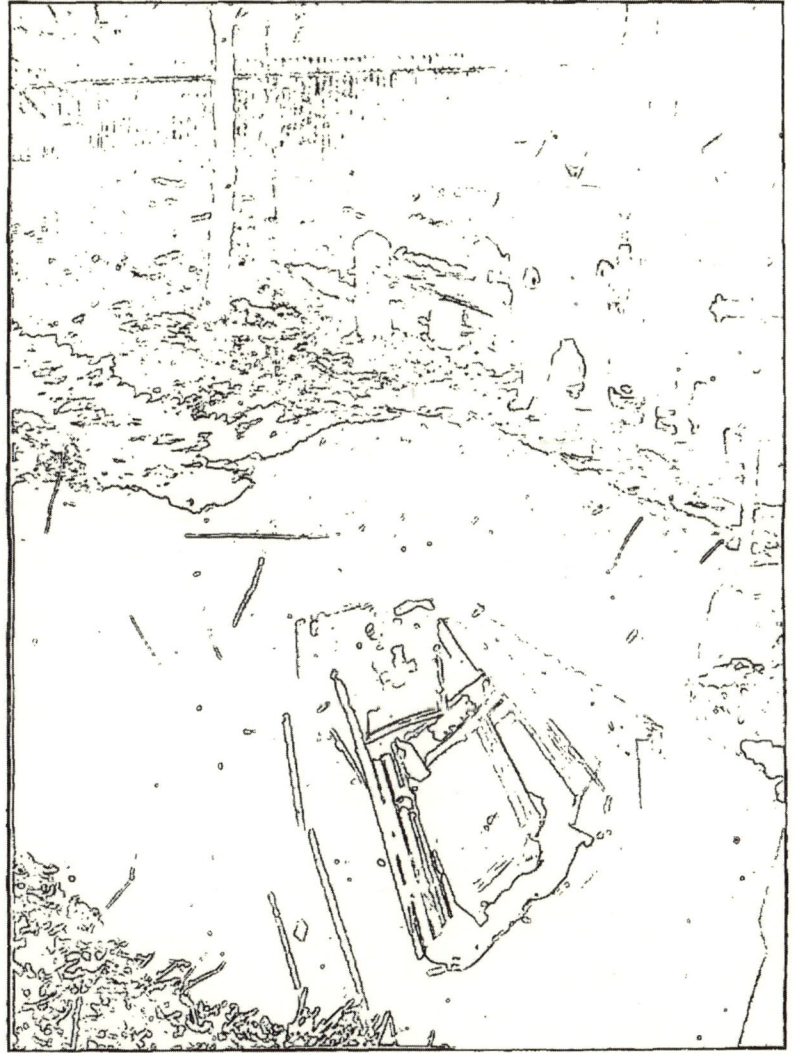

The last resting place of a well known Scranton, Pa., woman, whose grave was torn open, a few weeks after burial, by a mine cave, in Cathedral Cemetery, where hundreds of bodies have been dropped into the mine beneath. The casket is shown in the pit, torn asunder, and the hand of the corpse is seen protruding from the burial case.

SCIENTIFIC MANAGEMENT

a small part can't function
without connecting to another
it requires interlocking

note it with a stop-watch
equipped merely with a stop-watch
thousands of stop-watch observations
through the use of a stop-watch and record blanks
the man stood over him with a watch
the motion study followed by a minute study with a stop-watch
a man equipped merely with a stop-watch

the body is a cog
interpreted out of existence

breaking machines in the piece-work war
similar machines are made over and over again
every element of this machine
output doubled per machine
independent of work done by the machine
ten different experimental machines

a series of teeth on the side of a bar or wheel
cast as one with it
engaging with each other
precise sense doubtful
a great whele wyth many cogges
working trundles with round staves
locked to the surface and each other

"The 'psychological' prevents man from being as precise as a stopwatch; it interferes with his desire for kinship with the machine." (Dziga Vertov)

FONG FOO v. UNITED STATES

we submit, sir, that the risk of error or impropriety   must by borne

    Fong Foo who lost 15 pounds during the 13 days
the outburst of tears

I missed the trail, excuse me, sir

      one error   is an attempt to   psychoanalyze what the judge did

                             "I was going to take legal license
                             with Gertrude Stein and say 'An acquittal
                             is an acquittal is an acquittal,' sir."

recommended that they now thrust

                  a radiosonde
                  dropped from a plane by a parachute
as it passes through the air
returns to a receiver by Morse code

the temperature, the humidity, and the pressure of the air

              embodied the false testing

the judge's vigilance was particularly provoked
description of a test operation as resulting in spurious marks on a piece of paper
witness explained that spurious meant instantaneous, on the spur of the moment
the judge cautioned the witness

and then, the most important incident arose

1962. Standard Coil Products Company (with Fong Foo as a co-defendant) was accused of defrauding the government in connection with a multi-million dollar contract to supply weather monitoring equipment to the Army Signal Supply Agency. After seven days of what promised to be a long trial, the judge abruptly dismissed the case because of doubts concerning the credibility of the government's witnesses. Later, the government attempted to retry the case, but attorneys for the corporation claimed that the Fifth Amendment's statement "nor shall any person be subject for the same offense to be twice put in jeopardy of life or limb" applied to the defendant. The Court's decision affirmed that corporations were entitled to protection under the double jeopardy clause.

the situation arose which triggered the directed verdict

       riggered on the eighth day, after all this patience and indulgence

    dropped from an airplane
                    a parachute then opens
there is a certain shock at that point
        the parachute then allows the device to float to earth

the False Statements Act

it's difficult to describe those four or five days
they were—it was extremely long, extremely painful
the witnesses turned out to be rather inept

the witness must say that the signal would be dit-dit-da-da da-da-dit-dit

the judge objected to the word "chamber"
it might refer to a chamber pot

he objected to the use of the word "gave"
you must say he handed it to him

this use of the word "superiors"
an extraordinary malapropism

the witness had said he knew   it must be virgin hair
as one would speak of virgin timber or virgin wool
the judge   I think what he said need not be repeated

    he was just a technically educated man, ignorant of the English language

    it was an unfair slip of the tongue

I think this is the nub of it

"can" is a big word

the judge   simply turned off his ear

his cerebration is very rapid

we submit that words aren't that controlling

can this acquittal be tortured into a mistrial

"The word 'acquittal' in this context is no magic open sesame freeing in this case two persons and absolving a corporation from serious grand jury charges of fraud upon the Government." (Justice Clark, dissenting)

MALAPROPS

A pun is a word that forgets itself and behaves doubly.

It is the present and a man comes from the future. He has wires beneath his flesh. When he is shot, there are sparks and multicolored lights.

Electrical or electoral? Derangement or arrangement?

It is the present and a man dies one day but then is alive another day. Certain body parts that had been destroyed have been replaced by metals.

Spurious or superior? Flamingo or flamenco?

A man fights. At first he seems evil, but eventually he is proven good. He is a machine fighting other machines.

Illiterate or obliterate? Tantrum or tandem? Unanimous or anonymous?

A robot replaces a dead wife. She leads the workers to the machine halls to destroy the Heart Machine.

Malevolent or benevolent? Metal or mental?

A metal endoskeleton takes a pipe bomb to the abdomen. A metallic torso drags itself from an explosion. A mechanical man listens to his heartbeat.

Q. BURIED him! BURIED him, without knowing whether he was dead or not?
A. Oh no! Not that. He was dead enough.

The present. An enforcement droid escapes his monitors. He aims a neural spike at his residual humanity, his past organic form.

This happens again and again.

SIXTH AND SEVENTH AMENDMENT RIGHTS

ARMOUR PACKING COMPANY v. UNITED STATES

sixty-seven tierces of oleo oil

        false billing, false classifying, false weighing, false report

device

        a fine of not less than one thousand dollars nor more than twenty thousand dollars

    placed upon the like footing

a device   the term includes anything which is a plan or contrivance. Webster defines it to be "that which is devised or formed by design; a contrivance; an invention; a project," etc.

        the transportation was had, at least, in part in Kansas

this court held the crime to be a continuing one

this is a single, continuing offense

but this is a large country

1908. The Elkins Act required that all shippers be treated alike and that one rate be charged for similar types of freight. Armour Packing Company contracted with the Burlington Railway Company at the published rate at the time of the contract; their cargo was to go from Kansas City to New York, via Missouri. However, the rates changed between the time of the contract and its fulfillment. The packing company refused to pay the difference and was then convicted in Missouri for violating the Elkins Act. The company then claimed that since the "crime" they were accused of originated in

Kansas City, its trial by jury should have occurred there. The Court did not agree, but in its decision considered the corporate defendant an "accused" for Sixth Amendment purposes.

adding the ocean rate to the inland rate

the railroad carrier and the ocean carrier.

the ocean rate is uncertain and variable

to inform themselves as to the existence of the elements

punishing the shipper shocks my sense of justice

"Sustaining under those circumstances the power of the carrier and punishing the shipper shocks my sense of justice, and I cannot impute to Congress an intent by its legislation to make possible such a result." (Justice Brewer, dissenting)

ANIMALS 1

a rule is a rule

"All political and nationalist propaganda aims at only one thing; to persuade one set of people that another set of people are not really human…"
(Aldous Huxley)

bacteria, a virus
leeches, lice

parasites
subhuman vermin
large armed ants
dung flies
cockroaches

worms, lizards,
yellow rats
guinea pigs

stray dog, misguided dog, sly fox
cunning creatures
monkeys, apes, rodents

animal breath
two-legged animals who have mastered the technique of war
horns sprouting from temples
tails, claws, fangs

cargo

ROSS v. BERNHARD

ordinary breach
had it sued on its own behalf

                        the "dual nature"

            his claim   to be viewed as though it were
     the corporation itself

                                   this conceptualization

under the control of the wrongdoers

                          on behalf of the company

1970. Ross, a shareholder in the Lehman Corporation, alleged breach of contract, gross negligence, and fiduciary misconduct by the corporation's brokers and its Board of Directors. In his complaint, Ross asked the court for two forms of relief: 1) permission to file a derivative suit on behalf of the corporation and 2) money damages for the corporation's losses. Because the first is a matter of equity issue (for which there is no right to a jury trial), the question presented to the Court was whether the second form of relief (for which a jury trial in civil court was historically available) implicated a constitutional right to a trial by jury. The Court decided that the nature of the legal claims for damages triggered a right to a jury trial under the Seventh Amendment. Prior to this decision, a shareholder (i.e. a mouthpiece for company interests) had no right to a jury trial in derivative actions, regardless of the remedy sought. As a result of this decision, a plaintiff in a derivative suit has the same right to a jury trial as a corporation suing *on its own behalf.*

your Court's decision in Dairy Queen

                                    to temper the technicalities

                the common sense which controls laymen

the practical problems of life

                                      a creature of equity

that was the innovation that was brought about by Dairy Queen

                clear up that lack of parallelism

we cannot tell for sure what the Court thought

                              the controlling test
           the test of history

                is and always has been a creature

I hesitate to use the term

now, as I understand my friend's argument, it is that history must be reread or rewritten…

            that a man could bring a claim on behalf of another

Q: What is it the man's after…
A: Well, in this case, or the case of the complaint, the man is after money

           disgorge their profits   that is what he must do

the corporation is in hostile hands

a claim takes on a different coloration
has a completely different posture

Mr. Justice Holmes had before him the problem of whether there could be such an animal

        although an artificial being

    the Amendment and the Rules magically interact

"The fact is, of course, that there are, for the most part, no such things as inherently 'legal issues' or inherently 'equitable issues.' There are only factual issues, and, 'like chameleons [they] take their color from surrounding circumstances.' Thus the Court's 'nature of the issue' approach is hardly meaningful." (Justice Stewart, dissenting)

ANIMALS 2

follow the rules

"…if you are a high-priced man, you will do exactly as this man tells you tomorrow, from morning till night. When he tells you to pick up a pig and walk, you pick it up and you walk, and when he tells you to sit down and rest, you sit down." (Frederick Winslow Taylor)

he more resembles in his mental make-up the ox
he happened to be a man of the type of the ox
merely a man more or less of the type of the ox
heavy both mentally and physically

the endurance of the human animal
what fraction of a horse-power a man-power was
what fraction of a horse-power a man was able to exert
not more than one-eighth of a horse-power
half a horse-power of work

the horse-power which a man exerts
who stands still under a load is exerting no horse-power
he merely happened to be a man of the type of the ox
here is merely a man more or less of the type of the ox

a vertically crawling machine
could duplicate the lower animals
he stuttered his feelings and needs
like a starved and restless dog

FOURTEENTH AMENDMENT RIGHTS

SANTA CLARA v. SOUTHERN PACIFIC RAILROAD

Mr. Chief Justice Waite: The court does not wish to hear argument on the question whether the provision in the Fourteenth Amendment to the Constitution, which forbids a State to deny to any person within its jurisdiction the equal protection of the laws, applies to these corporations. We are all of the opinion that it does.

would place the organic law

in a position ridiculous to the extreme   to my mind, the fallacy

the Fourteenth Amendment refers to all persons without distinction

1886. Santa Clara County California sued the Southern Pacific Railroad for back taxes and the railroad refused to pay, claiming six different defenses. The railroad argued that the state had taxed them on fences they had built on county property, thus making their tax to the state unequal. In its decision, the Court agreed that the state didn't have the jurisdiction to tax the fence property and ruled in the railroad's favor. That would have been the end of it, except that one of the unused defense arguments was based on Fourteenth Amendment freedoms of equal protection for all persons. This Amendment had been created to grant equal protection to former slaves, but the railroad argued that it was also meant to protect corporations; if a corporation was a "person," local governments couldn't discriminate against it by having different laws and taxes in different places. This defense (and the seeming endorsement of the idea by Justice Waite's opening comment before the official opinion was delivered) was not addressed in the final decision, but somehow made its way into the court reporter's head note for the case. Although this head note is not legally binding, it was used as precedential evidence of the Fourteenth Amendment rights of corporations for years to come. There are many theories as to how this head note came to be, but no hard facts.

it is part of one sentence.

now, is it, can it be, a *judicial* question

    how much will disparage and distort

        for Defendants in Error, in consequence of an inquiry by a Member of the Court

by whatever name they are known; whether by the name of tribute, tithe, talliage, impost, duty, garble, custom, subsidy, aid, supply, excise, or other name

    the treasuries of despots

        prohibit tyrannical extractions

citizens may become subject to the unrestrained power of those who possess the machinery of government
            easy victims of every species of misrule

"[The Fourteenth Amendment's] mission was to raise the humble, the downtrodden, and the oppressed to the level of the most exalted upon the broad plain of humanity—to make man the equal of man; but not to make the creature of the State—the bodiless, soulless, and mystic creature called a corporation—the equal of the creature of God…" (Attorney for Santa Clara County, Delphin M. Delmas)

*

Note: In 1847 Abraham Lincoln, working for the Illinois Central Railroad, claimed that the railroad was a "person" and non-uniform taxation of different railroad properties was unfair and unconstitutional. After the Civil War, in an unsent letter, Lincoln wrote "As a result of the war, corporations have been enthroned and an era of corruption in high places will follow, and the money power of the country will endeavor to prolong its reign by working upon the prejudices of the people until all wealth is aggregated in a few hands and the Republic is destroyed. I feel at this moment more anxiety than ever before, even in the midst of war. God grant that my suspicions may be groundless."

Note: In the 1938 Supreme Court case Connecticut General Life Insurance Company v. Johnson, Justice Hugo Black's dissent stated "…of the cases in this Court in which the Fourteenth Amendment was applied during the first fifty years after its adoption, less than one-half of 1 per cent invoked it in protection of the negro race, and more than 50 per cent asked that its benefits be extended to corporations."

WE

Vertov: We foster new people. The new man...will have the light, precise movements of machines...

the heat of the heart is the mainspring
which can be felt with the fingers
bones are walls, beams, poles, keels

Vertov: Hurrah for the poetry of machines, propelled and driving; the poetry of levers, wheels, and wings of steel; the iron cry of movements...

veins are pipes
muscles and ligaments the foundations of a building

Vertov: And I make bold to slip them the ubiquitous mechanical ear and megaphone...

the stomach and the guts are another bigger pipe, dotted with many little holes
the skull is the roof, the head a warm factory

arteries are yet more pipes
these nerves fit to serve as instruments

elbows and knees are hinges on the door
vertebrae are a keystone in an arch
the spine is a vault

pneumatics, hydraulics, and all the other mechanicals
keep you safe (trapped)(overworked) within the building

Vertov: Come out, please, into life.

CHICAGO, MILWAUKEE AND ST. PAUL RAILWAY v. MINNESOTA

the transportation of milk

the prayer of the petition was that

I am frank to say it is hard to appreciate complaints from boards of trade

this, as usual, has been forgotten

this power of limitation

is itself without limit   this power to regulate   is not a power to destroy

to stay the hands

with the machinery provided by the wisdom of successive ages

1890. Minnesota had a rate-setting commission to govern railroad corporations that operated within the state. The Chicago, Milwaukee and St. Paul Railway Company refused to comply with the rates set by the commission on shipments of milk; the commission then asked the Supreme Court of Minnesota to force the railroad to lower its rates. The railroad, in response, asked to present evidence to the court to show that the commission's rates were unreasonable. The Minnesota court rejected the railroad's offer of evidence, so the railroad sought a review of that judgment in the Supreme Court, claiming that the situation deprived the company of its right to due process by law. The Supreme Court agreed with the railroad.

with all due deference to the judgment of my brethren

a manifest error hath happened to the great damage of the said respondent

a common carrier enjoys the right of way

two and one-half cents per gallon
three cents per gallon in ten-gallon cans

subjects the traffic in milk to undue and unreasonable prejudice

                          there is no plain, speedy, or adequate remedy

hereof fail not

given extraordinary powers and special rights

                must rely entirely upon the good faith of the people

the liability of a power to abuse is no argument against its existence

                      the wheels of government would often be blocked
                      helplessly entangled in the meshes of its own
constitution

the so-called railroad problem

our opinion is that the act is not obnoxious to the objection made

let the writ issue as prayed for

"There must be a final tribunal somewhere for deciding every question in the world. Injustice may take place in all tribunals. All human institutions are imperfect—courts as well as commissions and legislatures." (Justices Bradley, Gray, and Lamar, dissenting)

INDUSTRIAL PALACE

the body is a factory
in the workshop of the head

a suited one reads alone in the office of sensation
three argue around a table in the office of reason
a lab-coated one checks the dials in the gland center
two work the switchboard of the muscle center
three suited ones discuss the will

a group of persons are authorized to act as one
a group of persons combine in one body

the one at the ear has his ear to a wire
connected to a large web of sound
one stands behind the bellows camera of the eye
ready to pull the shutter

four at the switchboard of nerve central
nerves as telegraph
nerves as relay
nerves as electrical power lines

a group of persons as a tamed institution
a group of persons as secretly exerting power

breath
heartbeat
blood
a lab-coated one checks the levels
the marrow streams down from the nerves

a group of persons wrapped in the robes of legal sanction
a group of persons with immortality and limited liability

air is carried by pully and wheel
down from the nose to the lung
the sour stuff of oxygen
pistons, pipes, and turbines
property of the corporators

six at the table of the teeth
cutting, puncturing, sawing,
grinding, rolling, grating

further down the line
four in black convert sugar to starch
with the help of ladders they lift the blocks
onto the conveyor belt

a collection of individuals serve the greater good
a collective of persons serves profit only

the liver is a chemical plant
stomach and intestines a refinery
kidneys a filtering facility
dozens at the controls

a group of persons is private property
an association of individuals under an assumed name
sensory pathways as radio wires
brain as switchboard with operators

a group of persons like the feudal barons of old
troops of technicians manning the machines
a group of persons with the rights of citizens
an army of homunculi

a group of persons who can speak with one mind
a specialist works the gears

look at the body: it moves

TWO NOTES

1.

In my research, I came across this quote from legal scholar Frederic Maitland:
"[I]f n men unite themselves in an organized body, jurisprudence, unless it wishes to pulverize the group, must see $n+1$ persons."

Also this quote by political scientist Harold Laski:
"Just as we have been compelled by the stern exigencies of events to recognize that the corporation is distinct from its members, so, too, we have to recognize that its mind is distinct from their minds."

It occurred to me that such separation of the corporation from the individuals that make it up reanimates age-old ideas of a mind-body split. And I was struck at how this American "plus one" feels so threatening—like a monster—especially since the late nineteenth century, when corporate goals transitioned from serving the public good to serving profit only.

I thought about tales of resistance, how people can band together to fight against the odds. How a group of people can form a crowd, a surge, a wave. How the crowd can seem to have a mind of its own.

Must the plus one always be a monster?

2.
Pygmalion's Galatea, Dr. Frankenstein's monster, Olympia in E.T.A. Hoffman's "The Sandman," Delibes' Coppelia, Pinocchio, Hans Christian Anderson's mechanical bird, Kempelen's (and then Maelzel's) chess player. Automatons, puppets, cyborgs, robots, the uncanny valley. Mannequins, dummies, clockworks. Replicants, artificial intelligence, and Deep Blue. Objects pass the Turing Test. We are simultaneously attracted and repelled by the cognitive autonomy of our own creations: their immortality, their limited accountability, the impossibility of their imprisonment, their tendency to change citizenship overnight.

When the Supreme Court ruled in favor of Citizens United in 2010, there was an uproar. How could a corporation—a non-human entity—be granted the right of free speech? How could our Constitution protect corporations as if they were "of the people"? But the fact is, corporations have been collecting a variety of Constitutional rights since 1886. Their evolutionary leap from "artificial" to "natural" persons has been underway for more than a century.

An uneasy comparison whistles through, like a ghost. Two sides of an equation. A strained conditional.

If:

> With a corporation growing into maturity, there's definitely a sense of creative pride, but alongside that pride is a chill. Something complex and even alive has come into existence…a sort of mindless yet intelligent being. . .—Ted Nace, *Gangs of America*

Then:

> Living beings have been frequently and in every age compared to machines, but it is only in the present day that the bearing and the justice of this comparison are fully comprehensible.
> —Étienne-Jules Marey, *Animal Mechanism*

APPENDIX

AMENDMENT I
Congress shall make no law respecting an establishment of religion, or prohibiting the free exercise thereof; or abridging the freedom of speech, or of the press; or the right of the people peaceably to assemble, and to petition the government for a redress of grievances.

AMENDMENT IV
The right of the people to be secure in their persons, houses, papers, and effects, against unreasonable searches and seizures, shall not be violated, and no warrants shall issue, but upon probable cause, supported by oath or affirmation, and particularly describing the place to be searched, and the persons or things to be seized.

AMENDMENT V
No person shall be held to answer for a capital, or otherwise infamous crime, unless on a presentment or indictment of a grand jury, except in cases arising in the land or naval forces, or in the militia, when in actual service in time of war or public danger; nor shall any person be subject for the same offense to be twice put in jeopardy of life or limb; nor shall be compelled in any criminal case to be a witness against himself, nor be deprived of life, liberty, or property, without due process of law; nor shall private property be taken for public use, without just compensation.

AMENDMENT VI

In all criminal prosecutions, the accused shall enjoy the right to a speedy and public trial, by an impartial jury of the state and district wherein the crime shall have been committed, which district shall have been previously ascertained by law, and to be informed of the nature and cause of the accusation; to be confronted with the witnesses against him; to have compulsory process for obtaining witnesses in his favor, and to have the assistance of counsel for his defense.

AMENDMENT VII

In suits at common law, where the value in controversy shall exceed twenty dollars, the right of trial by jury shall be preserved, and no fact tried by a jury, shall be otherwise reexamined in any court of the United States, than according to the rules of the common law.

AMENDMENT XIV
SECTION 1.

All persons born or naturalized in the United States, and subject to the jurisdiction thereof, are citizens of the United States and of the state wherein they reside. No state shall make or enforce any law which shall abridge the privileges or immunities of citizens of the United States; nor shall any state deprive any person of life, liberty, or property, without due process of law; nor deny to any person within its jurisdiction the equal protection of the laws.

FURTHER READING:

George F. Deiser, "The Juristic Person," *University of Pennsylvania Law Review*, vol. 57, No. 3 (December 1908), pp. 131-142.

Thom Hartmann, *Unequal Protection*, Berrett-Koehler Publishers, 2010.

Gregory A. Mark, "The Personification of the Business Corporation in American Law," *University of Chicago Law Review*, vol. 54, No. 4 (Autumn 1987), pp. 1441-1483.

Carl J. Mayer, "Personalizing the Impersonal: Corporations and the Bill of Rights," 41 *Hastings Law Journal*, 577, 1989-1990.

Ted Nace, *Gangs of America: The Rise of Corporate Power and the Disabling of Democracy*, Berrett-Koehler Publishers, 2005.

The Oyez Project, www.oyez.org

Robert Sherrill, "Hogging the Constitution: Big Business & Its Bill of Rights," *Grand Street*, Vol. 7, No. 1 (Autumn, 1987), pp. 95-113.

Jeffrey Toobin, "Money Unlimited," *The New Yorker*, May 21, 2012, pp.36-47.

Other sources: Conrad William Cooke, *Automata Old and New*; "John Henry Blues"; Fritz Kahn, *Man Machine*; Charles Henry Olin, *Ventriloquism*; Frederick Winslow Taylor, *The Principles of Scientific Management*; Dziga Vertov, "We: Variant of a Manifesto" and "The Council of Three."

BIOGRAPHICAL NOTE

Jena Osman's recent books of poetry include *Public Figures* (Wesleyan Press, 2012) and *The Network* (selected for the 2009 National Poetry Series and published by Fence Books in 2010). Other books include *An Essay in Asterisks* (Roof Books) and *The Character* (Beacon Press). She co-edits the "Chain-Links" book series with Juliana Spahr, and teaches in the MFA Creative Writing program at Temple University in Philadelphia.

This book was computer typeset in Palatino with Optima titles by Rosmarie Waldrop. The cover was designed by Neil Cleary-Trask with an image by Amze Emmons. Printed on 60 lb. Nature's Recycled (an acid-free paper), smyth-sewn and glued into paper covers by McNaughton & Gunn in Saline, Michigan. There are 600 copies.